flux

a strategy guide

for OCD

This book is dedicated to any and all who have ever suffered from anxiety

introduction

The world is in a constant state of flux

The premise behind this book was derived from the pre-Socratic philosopher Heroclitus who boldly proclaimed that the world is in a constant state of flux and so it is impossible to achieve true knowledge of it. He is known for saying "You cannot step in the same river twice." In other words, us and the world are constantly changing. Therefore, what is true one moment is not necessarily true the next. There is a natural flow of energy in the world. Our anxiety becomes a non-factor, the more we are able to tap into this natural flow of energy.

The Big Three

Consistency, Reassurance, and Certainty are what I consider to be the three major triggers of obsessive-compulsive behavior. All of these irrational beliefs stem in some way or another from a need for certainty that no harm will come to us or the people we care about.

Breaking the thought cycles of The Big Three

This book is designed to help open your mind and expand your thinking. It is simply me sharing the concepts and ideas that have made my world less a place of rigid obsessive-compulsive behavior and more a place of flowing thought and creativity.

About me

In 1992, I was diagnosed with Obsessive-Compulsive Disorder. At the time I had no idea what it was but my suffering was so great that I was willing to do anything to lessen the severity. I knew I had to start at the beginning and so I decided to educate myself. I went to a used book store and bought every psychology textbook I could find. I read all of them into a cassette recorder and listened to them several times over the course of the next year or so.

Growing up I had a father who was constantly reading. Not a moment went by that he did not have a book or newspaper in front of him. With the advent of the internet his reading increased, only instead of books or a newspaper it was a computer. Furthermore, my grandfather also had a tremendous need for intellectual stimulation. In his spare time my grandfather would do algebra and geometry problems.

Shockingly, I was nothing like either my father or my grandfather until about age 26. In high school I had done poorly and did not find my schoolwork to be stimulating. In fact, I had little or no academic interests whatsoever. I am in some ways grateful for the onset of my OCD because it woke up something inside me. For the first time in my life I had a passion; and that was psychology.

Eventually, I went to college to study psychology further. I had always been interested in what makes people tick but what I had really wanted to know was if psychology could help me overcome my OCD. What I discovered is that it can but it takes a long time for it to be of any real use. First, I had to learn what was relative to me personally. Second, I had to discover through trial-and-error how to make it work.

This book is the pot beneath the strainer; it is a collection of the concepts which I feel are most relevant to OCD. Flux, is where the rubber meets the road between theory and personal experience; it is a fusion of personality psychology, moral philosophy, and the study of consciousness. I ask that you really spend some time with this book.

I do think you can make OCD a non-factor in your life.

"Just stop"

When you tell a therapist you are having the urge to carry out a compulsive act some may simply tell you not to; they may be unable to explain *how* to stop thinking about it. Indeed, they will respond with all sincerity by saying "When you have the urge to act out, just don't." There is nothing more frustrating than such an oversimplistic response to something which has made your life so incredibly painful. This book can explain to you the HOW behind the JUST DON'T.

It's all in the mindset

Alternatively, some therapists may suggest or script out certain cognitive-behavioral techniques to help condition you out of your OCD. Once again, attempting to overwhelm you with a plethora of specific responses for what is already a disorder of over-specificity is not a solution.

This book is a strategy guide on how to re-focus your attention until obsessions disappear on their own accord (rather than TRYING to ignore them away). Rather than address each individual obsession and compulsion with it's own technique (and become a one-armed paper hanger of short-term solutions) it is better to take a long-term approach. Flux is a way to challenge your thinking and make you less rigid. Namely, to help you develop an entire long-term strategy.

basic outline of my approach

Basically it works like this:

Whenever I become disconnected with myself I become disconnected with the world. I begin to copy the style of my critics. Because I live up or down to the expectations of others I begin to borrow their values rather than be my own person. Since I decide to 'not rock the boat' with those around me and live in accordance with their beliefs I fall into a state of **confluence**.

Confluence is also experienced as **depersonalization** (a feeling that one is floating above/looking down on their body and simply going through the motions of life).

What causes Confluence?

Confluence is caused from living in an inconsistent world. One minute mommy and daddy love me and the next minute they are yelling at me. Confluence has it's origin in mistrust. Since the only thing I can trust is what has worked for me in the past I will continue to repeat whatever behaviors won me approval. OCD is an attempt to bring consistency to an inconsistent world (e.g. - if I continue to do things this way, everything will be fine).

The opposite of Confluence

The opposite of Confluence is **Contact**. Contact is how I develop a genuine connection with the world. I am in contact when I use my five senses in order to process what is happening around me. As the gestaltists say, "Power is in the present" (live in the now). When I am able to rely completely on my present instincts I become part of the natural flow of life. Hence, I will process a first-person account of what I am presented with and respond in a way that is relevant. This process involves letting the natural me take over so that I may filter my life through personal/subjective experience instead of through the eyes of the critic (confluence).

Letting go of Confluence creates tension

When I let go of my need for approval from the critic it will generate tension. For a long time I have engaged myself in approval/reassurance-seeking behavior in order to relieve this tension. Therefore, when I cease to do this any longer what I have done is open the flood gates for the natural/ legitimate concerns of life to rush back in.

The good news is that tension is the glue that holds the world together; it is what brings people closer. When I can harness this tension it becomes a valuable source of emotional energy.

obsessional
uncertainty

I often talk with people about OCD when it is relative to a particular social circumstance. For example, I may tease someone about doing something that is kind-of obsessive-compulsive, which-in-turn may prompt a conversation on the subject. I have found that most people will half-heartedly declare themselves obsessive-compulsive in order to make this kind of light conversation. While engaged in laughter they may even gest that their husband or wife accuses them of it all the time. Most of the time, this is only a form of small talk that can be easily accounted for by behaviors that in actuality, are normal and un-intrusive to their daily lives. Nevertheless, many people do wonder at some point whether or not they are over-reacting in response to something they feel anxious about.

It raises an important question: How can we distinguish between what is normal and what is neurotic?

As a first step, I will start by defining what a rumination is.

The definition that I found to be the most concise is the one proposed by Padmal De Silva and Stanley Rachman in their book: "Obsessive Compulsive Disorder; the facts."

> A **rumination** is a train of thought, un-productive and prolonged, on a particular topic or theme....Unlike obsessions, ruminations do not intrude into the patient's consciousness, in a well-defined form, or a clearly circumscribed content. Clinically, it appears that ruminations are mental compulsive behavior, **usually preceded by an obsession**. For example, the obsession 'Am I going mad?' may lead to the compulsive urge to think through the subject, which in turn leads to a muddled attempt at thinking about it; this is the rumination....(**Mental compulsions**)....consist of specific mental acts, such as saying something si-lently or visualizing something in a particular way. Ruminations are not such well-defined events; the theme or topic of a rumination is specific, but what goes into the thinking about the topics are open-ended and variable. -DeSilva And Rachman

My belief about the theory of "Pure-O" is that it doesn't exist. Contrary to that belief, I DO NOT feel that you can be 100% obsessive without being mentally compulsive on some level. Re-member, even if you never physically carry out a compulsive act you are in your head still attempt-ing to rearrange things. Therefore, you are at the end of the day **still** being compulsive.

To be sure what an obsession is, lets look at the Diagnostic and Statistical Manual of Mental Disorders (DSM-IV-TR) to see what the criteria is for an obsession:

Obsessions - Recurrent, intrusive, and anxiety-provoking thoughts, impulses, or images.

Stage 1 -----> unspecific, open-ended (no resolution is decided on) = rumination

Stage 2 -----> specific (impulsive) resolution = physical/mental compulsion, similar to how a smoker reaches into a pack of cigarettes and lights up.

Stage 3 ---->takes steps to resolve the inner conflict (resists the urge for a cigarette).

Covert compulsions (mental compulsions) are repetitive thoughts designed to organize events through visualizing images or rehearsing silent strings of words. In a sense, it is a mental replacement for the physical act, or the condensing of many mental interpretations within a small timeframe.

In the movie, 'Two for the Money,' there is a scene where Al Pacino begins to verbalize the suspicious feelings he has about his wife and new employee (played by Matthew McConaughey). As he thinks out loud this introspection takes a turn for the worse, and before long his words sound increasingly jealous and paranoid. Finally, his wife played by Rene Russo interjects, "You are in your own head again. What'd I tell you about that? Stay out of there, its a bad neighborhood!"

I love that quote because it illustrates an important point. Namely, that a mental compulsion is a bad neighborhood. Yet we go there, again and again, like gluttons for punishment. We are like junkies driving downtown to cop a fix, without any regard for our safety, or whether we will get caught and arrested. What could we possibly need so bad? What is it that takes hold of our brains and forces us to navigate through endless cycles of disturbing obsessive-compulsive behavior? What are we really after?

The answer, of course, is: **the feeling of certainty/reassurance**. What makes the green grass, green? What makes a light switch, switched off? What makes a locked door, locked? Moreover, certainty and consistency go hand-in-hand and I'll discuss this later in the book.

Review

Rumination- Open-ended worrying with no attempt for a solution (worrying for the sake of worrying- chewing on something over and over).

Obsession- Recurrent, intrusive, and anxiety-provoking thoughts, impulses, or images.

Mental Compulsion- specific mental acts, such as thinking something or saying something silently to myself. It also can or visualizing or sorting something in a particular way.

Overt Compulsion- Physically carrying out the compulsive act. Can be checking to see if the door is locked or if the oven is shut off, etc.

contact

Reassurance Seeking

> Many of us resort to reassurance seeking, usually from members of our families. Often, obsessional thoughts such as 'Will I go insane?', 'Did I do it properly?', and 'Do I need to check the taps again?', lead to us asking for reassurance. When reassurance is received, the we feel some relief from our discomfort. Reassurance seeking is often done repeatedly, much to the exasperation of friends and family. At best, the provision of such reassurance only provides brief relief. -(DeSilva and Rachman)

There comes a point when no one can reassure us of anything. Ultimately, we must establish what our standards are and whether or not we live up to them. In other words, the template for what is real and what is not begins with us.

Even in the case of a compulsive act such as checking to see if the oven is shut off we must choose whether or not to believe what we are seeing at some point.

Don't ignore your obsessions

The worst thing anyone can do in life is tell you NOT to do something. This is because it will only make you want to do it more. So whatever you do, don't tell yourself to just stop. Rather, it is more effective to simply re-focus your energy in a on a solution, not on the problem. Hence, the obsessive-compulsive urges will go away on their own accord if and when you take the leap of faith that your re-focus itself is cure.

The How

In the beginning of this book I mentioned I would give you the 'How' answer to the question: How to just stop. Teaching you about the following will be part of this answer. I have mentioned the need for genuine contact with the world. It is a way to keep your mind actively engaged with your surroundings. The idea is to let yourself become stimulated by the people and places around you.

Suspension of disbelief

Stop trying to ignore your obsessions and mental compulsions. What happens whenever you try to ignore anything. You force yourself to notice it more. Rather, suspend these concerns, put them off until a more appropriate time (like you would put a virus in quarantine until you have a cure).

Maybe you are being irrational, and maybe realizing this works for you. Hence, you have ignored it already. But if something is nagging at you, and eating at your attention - and your ability to concentrate on your task, ignoring it has obviously become difficult. Do not invest any more energy in trying to prevent it. If it is an irrational concern, it will go away on its own accord if you continue to pay attention and focus in on what you are doing. There comes a point almost everyday where it is time to leave our personal thought life for a while and engage in a social one.

'Suspension of disbelief' is an idea that was devised by the poet and aesthetic philosopher Samuel Taylor Coleridge to justify the infusion of fantasy or non-realistic elements within literature. It is used to signify an implicit agreement that takes place between the writer and his audience. The writer provides a resemblance of truth and the reader agrees to suspend disbelief for the sake of entertainment. This allows the reader to engage him or herself in the story being told with an open mind. Moreover, this expression has been extended to include the genre of filmmaking, plays, etc.

Suspension of disbelief is something we do all do, all the time. Every time we watch a movie or TV program, or read a book, we undoubtedly suspend disbelief in some way. Therefore, we are already practicing this to some extent.

If while channel surfing one day, you find yourself watching Star Trek, you may notice a really ugly looking Klingon (with a really distorted looking face and an angry looking nose). It is an unreal presentation of a fictional creature; one that is hard to believe at first. Here there are these Klingons with these krinkily, angry looking faces (distorted and ugly) and they come from some planet (wherever that planet is). And perhaps there are Vulcans and other aliens. You suspend your disbelief as to whether or not something like this could ever exist. Perhaps because you become interested in the story that is being told.

In his book "Brain Lock," Dr. Jeffrey Schwartz recommends waiting at least fifteen minutes before carrying out a compulsion, if you decide that you are going to.

> The idea is to delay your response to an obsessive thought or to your urge to perform a compulsive behavior by letting some time elapse - preferably at least fifteen minutes - before you even consider acting on the thought....Then you must do another behavior - any pleasant, constructive behavior will do. -Jeffrey Schwartz

Once you have begun to delay/suspend your response to your urge to be obsessive-compulsive (for 15 minutes) you will need to decide *what* to re-focus your attention on. Why not focus on what is happening around you at that moment?

Tension

Once I decide to let go of the security blanket of confluence (need for approval) I have been carrying around I can begin to feel.

> Tension has its own directional power.... What had previously been choked off, cast into the past, becomes reborn now through the currently available sensory and motor realities....Completion emerges through recognition, enhancement and continuing focus until motor discharge - available only in the present – finally releases the person from living in the dead past....any return to present experience is in itself a part of the antidote to neurosis. -Polster & Polster

The first way to make contact with the world is to use my 5 senses: Smell, Touch, Taste, Hearing and Seeing. Whenever I restrict my world (reduce my awareness) in order to create a more ordered existence (one without risk) I cut myself off from the natural flow of the world.

> Contact is not just a togetherness or joining. It can only happen between separate beings, always requiring independence and always risking capture in the union. At the moment of union, one's fullest sense of his person is swept along into a new creation.... (but also) ....A special aspect of contactfulness comes from the possibility of being in contact with oneself.... because of the human ability to split oneself into the observer and the observed. - Polster and Polster (1978).

A little tension is a good thing

It's healthy to feel that underlying tension during my interactions with others. It keeps me alert and in tune with what is taking place in the present. I prefer to think of unresolved tension as the glue that holds us all together. Moreover, it is that glue which keeps me attentive to my environment and out of my head obsessing.

The world is not completely safe and secure and never will be. In this world there will be those who are trustworthy and those who aren't. There will always be some level of unresolved tension underlying my interactions with others. I can choose to be alert to these risks (contact) or be a recluse for the rest of my life who has fallen into protection mode (Confluence/OCD). One thing is for certain, OCD is not the solution.

how to make contact

Pacing

Pacing means meeting the other person where he or she is, reflecting what he or she knows or assumes to be true, or matching some part of his or her ongoing experience [...] The words, phrases, and images other people use give you important information about the inner worlds they inhabit. By pacing this aspect of their speech, you are telling them that you understand them and that they can trust you. - JerryRichardson

Aiming my focus

Pacing requires that you actively listen to what another person is saying. If you are standing in their shoes and attempting to see things from their point of view. As they talk you notice the speed and depth at which the conversation is taking place. If you ask someone how they are doing and their answer is a short one which does not contain much information then it becomes obvious they are moving at a slow pace. Conversely, if their answer is long and informative you are moving at a faster pace.

Conversational turn-taking

Another subtler and slightly differentiated version of pacing is what is known as conversational turn-taking. The idea stems from Harvey Sacks' work on conversation analysis.

Sack's analysis of both storytelling and telephone calls reveals the mutual monitoring of each other's turns which is basic to sequential organization of conversation....in hearing how what they have just said is heard, speakers discover from recipients' responses what they have taken to have intended to mean.

At times, without consciously realizing it, people may exercise too much control over their conversations with others. We have all known people like this. Even after they have made their point clear, they still continue to talk. In fact, they may automatically jump to the next point without even stopping to let you comment on the previous one. Conversational turn taking is a skill learned early in life and in fact, some people never develop it at all.

When caught up in obsessive-compulsive activities, the fine art of pacing and conversational turn-taking get lost in the shuffle. Nevertheless, they are powerful tools that can be used to break the obsessive-compulsive cycle. They can help you to get out of your head and back to your present surroundings.

Staying in contact mode

There is no such thing as not communicating. In fact, the evidence of what and how people anchor their experiences surround us all the time in the form of body language.

> People can communicate different types of information at different levels of understanding. The communication process consists of more than the spoken or written language [...] Feedback plays a major role in the full communication process, and gesture clusters are an important feedback. They indicate from moment to moment and movement to movement exactly how individuals or groups are reacting nonverbally. If we subconsciously conceive of the gesture as unfriendly, without conscious control we bring about a belligerent reaction that degenerates in to a vicious cycle of hostility.
> -Nierenberg and Calero

Gerald Nierenberg and Henry H. Calero's "How to read a person like a book" was published in 1971. They gave seminars on how to read body language in order to help give others a glimpse at this underlying style of communication. In their book they talk about gestures, clusters of gestures, postures, congruency. There are things that people do automatically without their realizing it.

-When a person is running her hand through her hair...this is getting in her hair

-When someone has his hand on his neck...this topic is a pain in their neck

-When we have our arms crossed we may be turning inward to process information (and shielding ourselves in the process)

-A person may pull on their ear, if they don't want to hear it

-Sometimes we restrain ourselves from talking by grasping our arm, or pressing our finger against our lips to keep them shut Etc, etc.

This book will open up a whole new world of communication for you. Because once you begin to notice these little non-verbal gestures, you can switch gears between your thoughts and social interactions smoothly.

Sub-communication

By now you understand there is a level of sub-communication that can be interpreted by watching your body language. Of course, this style of sub-communication will take place whether or not you are speaking actual words. Conversely, there are layers of sub-communication which do underlie your words and actions. For example, the mere fact that you understand and use the concepts of pacing and conversational turn-taking will sub-communicate confidence and assertiveness.

Basically, sub-communication is who you are. It is that person who will continue to surface no matter how directly you attempt to communicate otherwise. The more your behavior contradicts your direct communication the greater the sub-communication. For instance, someone who tries to outwardly appear confident yet acts out of desperation will ironically sub-communicate insecurity. Someone who attempts to communicate independence yet is loud and boisterous may sub-communicate a need for attention. Someone who attempts to communicate trust yet endlessly questions a lover as to their whereabouts will sub-communicate a lack of trustworthiness.

Life is a series of resets where we must constantly shift gears out of one state and into another. Whenever we fall into a rut or find ourselves rumination/obsessing it's time to reset and once again focus on the processing speed of the others sharing our environment. Consider the following poem as an anecdote.

living in the reset

won't try to ignore
or invest anymore
than i need to
forget
focus is a reset
moving
picture mindset
back to the now
embracing
conversational
turn-taking
pacing
the changing
truth
every moment is new
and i can do
anything

Review

The basis behind my theory is that OCD/anxiety stems from a lack of consistency (which causes mistrust and therefore, a need for constant reassurance).

So far I have discussed the concepts of Contact and Confluence and why I feel they are important to understanding anxiety. The idea is to establish and maintain a physical contact with my environment based solely on the use of my five senses. By practicing how to fully utilize my five senses I will begin to establish a consistency with how I interact with my surroundings; whereupon, I become less reliant on my OCD (habits of confluence) to establish this sense of consistency.

I am no longer observing; instead i'm on the playing field and back in the game. The next step is to know where I am going. I need a map to help navigate the terrain. Doing this will require some soul-searching. What do I want out of life? What is my main goal? What will I need to learn along the way to reach this goal?

destination: highest good

Virtues

I need a highest good, it's that simple. My-highest good is something I can discover only through soul-searching.

Basically, it works like this: If the highest good I aim for in life is worthy enough I will need to learn/achieve several virtues along the way in order to achieve it. There are several virtues which have been delineated throughout the course of history; we will look at only a few for the purpose of illustrating the main point of this chapter.

A virtue is the mean between two extremes; the balance or temperance of a character trait. For example, Courage is the mean between Cowardice and Rashness.

Here are some examples:

Courage - (Cowardice/Rashness)
Temperance - (Insensibility/Intemperance)
Modesty - (Shamelessness/Bashfulness)
Right Ambition - (Want of Ambition/Over-ambition)
Wittiness - (Boorishness/Buffonery)
Sincerity - (Ironical Depreciation/Boastfulness)

The point here is a simple one: Choose a highest good. If your highest good is to be a clinical psychologist you can imagine a general idea of the path it would take to reach that goal.

Many virtues will need to be explored and achieved in order to reach this highest good. You will need money for school, good grades, career choices, etc. Consider each step along the way to your highest good. Once you do that, you will have a map to work with.

In the end we only hit what we aim at. It's not personality change itself that we are focused on. We are simply making it a point to re-focus strongly and creatively in one direction.

anxiety

Starting point

You have now reached your starting point; You are ready to begin. I will call where you are now, Point A. Your destination involves being actively engaged with your environment and not relying on the approval of others (this is about you). The journey (time frame) between Point A and your destination may be a great one. As a rule, you increase your anxiety in proportion to the goals you set for yourself and the time frame required to achieve it. Therefore, you have created the potential for much anxiety. Your goal is to not rely on old habits for dealing with the tension this will cause. Keep taking in the world through your five-senses as your own person.

Zone of proximal development

The psychologist Lev Vygotsky who is known for his work in child development, used the term **scaffolding** to describe this process of borrowing a support structure to further an individual's personal development. Only, he took it a step further and introduced the concept of the "Zone of proximal development." Basically, this term describes what a person can or cannot do without the assistance of a scaffold or mentor. Also, it suggests that it may take some a greater or lesser amount of time to accomplish.

Scaffolding

In order to establish a healthier set of coping mechanisms which stem entirely from myself I will first need a scaffold (support structure) to sustain me during this growth period.

The word scaffolding describes what painters refer to as a raised wooden or metal platform attached alongside a building. It is on this platform that painters or construction workers work their magic. Interestingly enough, it is also been known to describe a platform used for public executions.

When I re-focus my attention from the constant nagging for reassurance to the fresher, more lively energy available only in the present, the unhealthy aspects of my personality fade to the background and no longer have any real bargaining power. It is sort of like I am both replacing and re-arranging the philosophical furniture of my thought life simply by giving my re-focus a head start.

It's important to understand what Anxiety is

Anxiety is the driving force that takes me from where I am now to where I want to be. There are many ways of defining anxiety. Indeed, its definition has grown into an art-form. Nonetheless, sooner or later you are going to have to pick a definition to use, and then put it to the test. Gradually, you can modify your ideas, but you have to start somewhere.

Rollo May

Rollo May, the existential psychologist, believed that anxiety is associated with creativity and is not necessarily a bad thing to have. He understood that we must take advantage of the freedom we have to harness this energy. In particular, he said that man is the only creature that is conscious of the fact that he will someday die, and out of this comes normal anxiety.

May believed, along with the other existentialists, that the most important fact about humans is that they are free. As we have seen, however, freedom does not produce a tranquil life. Freedom carries with it responsibility, uncertainty, and therefore anxiety....Neurotic anxiety is not conducive to personal growth because it results from the fear of freedom.

One of the things that I like about May's perspective is that it not only nicely defines what anxiety is, it also provides a constructive solution. "Freedom is the mother of all anxiety," he said. "We're aware that what we do matters, and that we only have about seventy or ninety years in which to do it, so why not do it and get joy out of it."

Creating yourself

So the point to this chapter is this: Enjoy the process of re-creating yourself into a healthier person and allow yourself a reasonable amount of time to do it. Otherwise, you will rush the process and your anxiety will go through the roof. And what happens when your anxiety hits the roof? You seek to alleviate the uncomfort of that over-whelming anxiety through the emotional retreat of obsessive/compulsive behavior. None of this will ever work if you simply move your current obsessive agenda over to this. If you obsess about getting better you haven't accomplished anything.

Review

-The secret in managing anxiety is in developing a consistent way of interacting (and connecting) with the world on a personal (well-tempered) level.

-Practice the use of the five senses and how to actively use them while interacting with the world in order to establish and maintain a healthy focus.

-Once I begin to no longer rely on the approval of others for a sense of reassurance I will need to become my own source of strength and confidence (or sense of consistency). Inevitably, I will need to answer the question "Who am I and where am I going?" in order to do this.

-The first step in answering the question "Who am I?" is to know where I am going (Choose a main goal/highest good). If my highest good (or main goal) is a worthy one it will require the practice of several virtues in order to achieve it. Life is a journey and the journey itself is what makes it interesting.

-Once I set this goal (aim towards a highest good) there will be a certain amount of anxiety. Anxiety can lead to creativity if properly maintained (a little tension is good). If not properly maintained it can lead to shallow living where I constantly micromanage my time (and thereby miss the whole point of the journey of self-creation).

-In order to establish a healthier set of coping mechanisms which stem entirely from myself I will first need a scaffold (support structure) to sustain me during this growth period. Scaffolds can be anything that inspire spiritual/personal growth but ultimately, must be processed within a personal/relevant context and filtered by personal experience.

Anxiety - **A**nxiety comes from the space between where we are now and where we want to be. If right now I work at Wendy's - but within the span of the next six months I want to write a book, sell millions of copies, and buy a boat to sail around the Caribbean with - I am going to have a lot of anxiety. For the most part, anxiety is healthy. It gets us up off the couch and striving to achieve something. Anxiety only becomes unhealthy when we try to accomplish too much, too soon.

the
chemicals
of
certainty

Mental and physical interaction

Obviously, there are some chemical components involved with the onset of OCD. The question is can I change my body chemistry if I change my decision-making processes. Conversely, if I change my decision-making processes do I also change my body chemistry?

Repeating something until it becomes unconscious

One example would be a cigarette smoking addiction. It is a mental choice to start smoking; no one physically forces me to do it. Furthermore, it is a choice that changes my body chemistry. An addiction develops from what begins as a series of conscious choices: Everytime I feel the urge for a stress release regardless of the reason, I light a cigarette. Once I have done this a certain amount of times it becomes an unconscious process (or habit). The personality is a combination of many consciously-made decisions which have been repeated until they become unconscious. I am an efficient creature and will seek to maximize my thought capacity by letting some behaviors become automatic. I can only keep so many things in my immediate awareness. Eventually auto-pilot takes over the operations I am most used to performing. The paradox is that even though this makes me more efficient, it also serves to make me less conscious.

A habit is a mental cigarette

A mental/overt compulsion is a **mental cigarette** that results from the obsessional urge for a chemical boost. Only, instead of that desire for a chemical boost being one for nicotine as it is with the cigarette smoker, it is for the OCD-sufferer a desire for consistency, reassurance, and certainty. So it stands to reason that if I stop smoking I will lose the dependency for certainty and reassurance. However, just as the task of becoming a non-smoker is not easy neither will be the process of developing new habits.

At some point it becomes obvious: I believe a habit will help me to be a more efficient person. Perhaps that very first time I carried out a mental/overt compulsive act I saw that it reduced anxiety. Consequently, I decided to use it as a coping mechanism. Because checking the oven gave me a feeling of reassurance and because emotions are some of the most addictive chemicals there are, the next time I needed a feeling of reassurance I decided to once again check the oven. If we carry out this sequence of cause and effect enough times we will begin to associate checking the oven with reassurance until it becomes unconscious. Like any other addictive behavior I eventually build a tolerance and have to check more than once.

Mental cigarettes everywhere

It stands to reason that OCD is a living nightmare of illusory cause and effect relations. (E.g. - If I do this in such a way, everything will be fine). Of course it is not a real solution, never was. Like cigarettes, OCD is a coping mechanism. I have taught myself to believe it works for me. So, is it really hard to believe that I can develop **new** healthier cause and effect relationships to replace it? When you think about it... no, it really isn't. Nevertheless, it takes a larger than life effort; one that starts with a new sequence of conscious choices.

Nicotine patch

Just as some may decide to use a nicotine patch to ween themselves off their nicotine addiction, I can use a certainty patch to ween me off the need for certainty/reassurance. The key here is to not use the patch forever; it is simply a scaffold or psychological boost. This is exactly what the idea of a scaffold is that I have been talking so much about.

I have to breathe my own life into whatever information I absorb through the trial and error of my own five senses. Once it has been filtered through my personal experiences it will finally crystallize.

How the body adjusts to a belief

So far I have used the idea of "The mental cigarette" to describe how a belief translates into habit. In addition, I have shown that choosing to develop this habit will change my body chemistry.

Belief: If I smoke a cigarette, I will feel better.

Habit: I smoke cigarettes to feel better.

Body Chemistry: Psychological and Physical dependency on cigarettes.

OCD/Anxiety

Belief: If I do this a certain way everything will be fine. (E.g. If I make sure the door is locked I will protect myself from harm).

Habit: I make sure the door is locked to protect myself from harm.

Body Chemistry: A feeling/emotion is a chemical. I feel safe (certainty fix).

Wait, why am I doing this again?

Again, once a habit becomes unconscious I may forget why I do it. One day while checking to see if a door is locked (over and over again) I may find myself thinking: **why am I checking this lock over and over again? I already know it is locked yet I keep checking.** As I'm walking away: **wait, am I sure it was locked? Maybe I should check again.**

Stop the press, someone should call a scientist

Yea, scientists know. In his book "The Biology of Belief "(2005), Bruce Lipton writes about the work he has done with cloning cells and what he found is genes alone are not the determinants of gene traits. Wait, say that again?

It works like this:

-Genes are only a blueprint; they only become activated if/when they are read. Genes are read when the DNA has been exposed to signals from the environment. My perceptions shape/filter how my cells will convert that information into action.

> To exhibit "intelligent" behavior, cells need a functioning membrane with both receptor (awareness) and effector (action) proteins. These protein complexes are the fundamental units of "perception." The definition of perception is "awareness of the elements of environment through physical sensation. - Bruce Lipton

Belief in a habit = Body Chemistry

In other words, the cellular membrane is that place where my beliefs connect with my body chemistry. If I was to break it all down and attempt to explain it all in terms of science this is the direction I would take it.

Review

-Habits serve as a vehicle to consistency. They start as conscious decisions and after several repetitions they become unconscious. The cause and effect relationship (or reason for performing the habit) becomes unconscious as well.

-OCD/Anxiety is a coping mechanism (habit) that I have taught myself to use.

-Habits/Beliefs = Chemicals

-Perceive something for long enough and your cells will align themselves with your perceptions.

cognitive map

Give yourself props

Imagine moving somewhere that you have never been before. Now imagine, that your job requires you to take several different routes to work at times because of frequent traffic jams and car accidents. Your first payday arrives, and you find out that your job prints pay checks that must be cashed in person at a bank located outside of town. It's Friday and you really want that money! You have driven through that part of town twice before, but you were tired, and busy running many errands, so your memory is a little fuzzy. But you have that check in your hand and you are ready to put your memory to the test.

In your mind, you replay the events that took place during the first two trips you made to this part of town and begin to remember several landmarks along the way. First, you remember that you made a right at a McDonalds because it had a really big play area in front, and there were many kids running and jumping around. Second, you remember that you made that first left after crossing the gray stone bridge. You specifically remember this because of a kid that scared you half to death - by darting out onto the road in front of you on his bike - in order to race across the street before you could complete your turn.

Edward Tolman, once did a study based on a very similar proposal of memory. He put rats in a T-maze and observed how well they remembered their way around by first letting them navigate themselves out without giving them any specific motivation to do this. After days of trial runs he rewarded the rats with food when they completed the maze.

As an example, when an animal is first placed in the start box of a T-maze, the experience is entirely new, and therefore the animal can use no information from prior experience. As the animal runs the maze, it sometimes turns right at the choice point and sometimes left. [...] If the earlier hypothesis "If I turn left, I will find food" is confirmed, the animal will develop the expectancy "When I turn left, I will find food." If the expectancy is consistently confirmed, the animal will develop the belief "Every time I turn left in this situation, I will find food." Through this process, a cognitive map of this situation develops-an awareness of all possibilities in a situation.

Basically, Tolman noticed that the rats made fewer errors on days they were rewarded as opposed to the days they were not rewarded. Therefore, he concluded that the rats must have used a "cognitive map" that they had developed previously, during the trial runs (the times they had not received a reward). He felt that the rats used this cognitive map as a reference to run the maze in a shorter time, in order to receive as many rewards as possible. Hence, the idea of the cognitive map.

The initial learning that occurred during the no reward trials was what Tolman referred to as latent learning. He argued that humans engage in this type of learning everyday as we drive or walk the same route daily and learn the locations of various buildings and objects. Only when we need to find a building or object does learning become obvious. Controversy developed from Tolman's theory of latent learning, but several investigators demonstrated that rats do learn in the absence of rewards.

Moral Compass

> The noble type of man experiences itself as determining values; it does not need approval; it judges, "what is harmful to me is what is harmful in itself"; it knows itself to be that which first accords honor to things; it is value-creating.
> - Friedrich Nietzsche

Love this quote from Friedrich Nietzsche because I feel it so adequately describes the process of self-discovery. If I want to truly know who I am, I have to create myself like an artist creates a masterpiece. Consequently, I must face the reality of where ever this creation takes me. In order for me to be in contact with the world **I must** develop an understanding of this from a first-person perspective. This is because a moral compass **can only** be developed in the first person. It must be breathed in through my five senses and filtered through my personal experience (the legitimate suffering of trial-and-error).

A moral compass is what I use to navigate myself through the territory of my life. In order to have a functional moral compass I need to be fearless about owning up to what it is and what is not in my best interest.

Legitmate suffering

> Neurosis is always a substitute for legitimate suffering. - Carl Jung

Adolescence is nothing but a jump off phase of development where I am discovering my independence from my parents and authority figures. Even though there are certain personality traits, mannerisms, and values, that I inherit from my parents, some of these may or may not be of any use to me in my adult life. Indeed, as a teenager I knew all too well the process of legitimate suffering (growing pains). Another thing to understand about legitimate suffering is that it involves **delaying of gratification**. Specifically, putting off the pleasures of life until responsibilities are taken care of.

Rite of passage

In high school I identified with certain social groups to see where I fit in. Although I initially looked at what the groups were doing as a whole, I know this was only a temporary phase (a scaffolding/temporary pattern of recognition). It was simply a sequence of events I had to experience in order to see how I fit personally within a social context. The adolescence phase is particularly painful because of the growing pains involved in this process. However, it is through the exercise of my own set of morals that I can develop real intimacy with the world and my relationships.

psychology for the progressive mind

silence..
speaking begins with
listening
to the allure of
your own
imperfection
otherwise
what is the point
of reflection

even a lie
becomes what is true
in itself
about you
it is for irony
alone to decide
which literal intentions
to hide

chances are
whatever
escaping truth
does exist
it most likely resides
within this
endless completing force
of the will
where
self-deception
is only grist for the mill

Review

Cognitive Map - My cognitive map is a representation of my past, present, and future experiences. It is interesting way to guage where I am on the way to my highest good. It is where I am in the process of discovering how I fit into the world.

Moral compass- My moral compass is how I navigate myself through the right and wrong/do's and dont's of life. Specifically, it is my first-person account of what is right and wrong which I acquire through my own personal trial-and-error.

Legitimate suffering- The first step to understanding how to navigate myself through life with my own value system is to understand the growing pains involvd in the trial-and-error process. Any attempts to avoid this necessary path to growth will lead to a lack of contact with the world. Legitimate suffering also involves delaying of grafication. Part of discovering who I am is putting in the time it takes to achieve the goals I wish to reach. If I never make the necessary sacrifice of putting aside what is immediately gratifying for something long-term, how will I know if I can accomplish it?

when the map
is not the
territory

Practicing imperfection

In the previous section I gave an example of how you might construe a cognitive map (mental representation) based on past events, as Tolman suggested. The kid speeding across the street on his bike represented an immediate danger and as a result, it became a landmark, which may turn out to be accurate the next time you pass through this area. Conversely, the McDonald's landmark may be largely inaccurate. You may not notice this until you are at one of three intersections with a McDonalds (all of them with play areas in front). There are too many McDonald's restaurants with play areas! Therefore, doing what you did before may not help you. In fact, you may end up going out of your way and getting completely lost. The map was not the territory!

Some parts of your map may indeed, be accurate at times. But the point is that you have to take into account the distortions that come about from your misconceptions and limited accuracy. Not to mention the circumstances which can innacurate or obsolete something that was once valid.

> We are daily bombarded with new information as to the nature of reality. If we are to incorporate this information, we must continually revise our maps, and sometimes when enough new information has accumulated, we must make very major revisions. The process of making revisions, particularly major revisions, is painful, sometimes excruciatingly painful. And herein lifes the major source of many of the ills of mankind. -Scott Peck

Depression

At times it becomes necessary to give up things in life which no longer have a place in our lives. Most often, whenever I am feeling depressed about something it prompts the question: How important is this to my life? Is it interfering with what is most important to me?

Ways of responding to the world which were appropriate at one time may no longer be appropriate now. Therefore, it becomes necessary to revise my map. For example, my cognitive map changes a great deal if/when I make the transition from a single person to a married person. Certain behaviors that served me well as a single man may no longer have a place in my life. Of course, it opens the way for newer, more relative changes to my behavior. Fatherhood is another example of a transition that will require me to give certain things up.

at the speed of depression

i think
therefore i am
the observer effect
i plan
has a few
drawbacks

when i won't
remain the same
self-image
begins
to change
i let it die
i let it die

the obsolete
becomes my rift
depression is my gift
progressive
as it is
it gets me high

and when
the past is gone again
i let it die

Alfred Korzybski is the Polish-American scientist and philosopher who remarked, "The map is not the territory." Basically what Korzybski meant is that neither an abstraction derived from something, or a reaction to it, is the thing itself. You can drop a brick on your foot and feel pain from the brick, but this pain doesn't necessarily tell you what the brick is made of. You cannot derive what the internal structure of the brick is based on the pain that you feel.

I may develop a basic mental representation of Orlando but it is not Orlando, itself. It is as filtered and distorted as my attention span allows it to be - and only the stimulus that is unique enough to stand out will actually register.

A map and no compass

Trying to navigate through the cognitive territory of my life without a moral compass (used within the context of legitimate suffering) will sidetrack me into territory which does not accurately represent who I am.

I go into ideas such as Pacing, Conversational Turn-taking, and Sub-communication because they keep us in tune with the natural progression of things and help us to accurately guage where we are in relation to the world.

Depersonalization

When I don't allow myself to take in the world through the first person and instead live by the values of my critics I will feel detached (and be in a state of confluence) with the world. Many people experience this as a form of depersonalization. Contrary to popular belief, people with OCD do experience depersonalization. While interacting with others some may find themselves simply going through the motions of a personality, not their own. As a bi-product, they don't seem to be tapped in emotionally to what is happening to them. Life has become a series of shortcuts designed to avoid legitimate suffering. Their capacity to delay gratification (put business/responsibility before immediate gratification) becomes non-existent and they begin living life on fast forward.

> The feeling of continuity of consciousness is critical for maintaining one's sense of personal identity. Serious **depersonalization** would result if, each time you awoke, you could recall nothing of the events of the previous day. Exactly this sort of depersonalization occurs in cases of severe anterograde amnesa, in which brain-damaged patients are unable to transfer new information-including memories of personal experiences-from working memory to long-term memory.
> -William Farthing

Depersonalization = Inconsistency

Confluence describes what I believe to be a huge problem for us all who suffer from severe anxiety. Specifically, the stereo-typed, cultist behavior of an imitator, who feels seperated from his/her own body. Many OCD sufferers claim to experience spells of depersonalization where they feel disconnected from themselves, as if they are simply going through the motions of a life that is not really theirs.

Confluence leads to depersonalization precisely because you cannot foster a real sense of contact (and develop a real sense of consistency) with the world if you are simply doing and saying what you see others doing and saying. For example, my father was an avid reader of movie critics when I was growing up. When I would see the previews for a movie on TV and expressed interest in seeing the movie he would inevitably respond with how a local critic has reviewed the movie. Baffled, I would respond "Who cares what the critic says?" There is only one way to find out if I like the movie and that is to see it myself.

Imagine a personality built solely on outward appearance. One designed to show off one's knowledge and distract from distrusted feelings; that is what depersonalization is. It is a feeling of self-awareness I get when I am not real and the things happening to me lack personal significance.

The observer effect

How does depersonalization start? Werner Heisenberg, the German theoretical Physicist introduced the idea of the uncertainty principle, and the resulting, observer effect. According to Heisenberg, the accuracy of your observations are inversely proportional to the position that you are making them from in that particular moment in time.

In other words, not only am I limited to the information that I presently have available to me, but that information changes as I observe it! This is similar to Korzybski's observation; and just as Korzybski points to the potential for "Obsessional-map-making," so Heisenberg can help me to understand this as well. Sometimes I inadvertently create sub-obsessions while observing myself, and as a result I sidetrack myself.

The German physicist Werner Karl Heisenberg found that the very act of observing an electron influences it's activity and casts doubt on the validity of the observation. Heisenberg concluded that nothing can ever be known with certainty in science. Translated into psychology, this principle says that, although human behavior is indeed determined, we can never learn at least some cause of behavior because in attempting to observe them we change them....Such a position is called **indeterminism.**

Once I begin to measure what my position is, I have changed it. If I am not really worried about this, then why do I keep thinking about it? And so, not only has my concern become an obsession but I now have a second obsession running parallel with the first.

The danger often lies in trying to find the quick fix, the instant certainty that I am right, and that everything is OK, so that my anxiety will be relieved.

It is always tempting to take the gamble that I can resolve an internal conflict - by splitting my consciousness, plugging in a quick rationalization - through a mental compulsion - and stepping right back into the shoes of my present awareness. Not only is this not a good idea for reasons that I gave above, but I am taking a huge gamble by doing this.

At the point that I split my consciousness, I roll the dice. I am in a sense betting on the odds that I can resolve my compulsive urge quickly enough to not miss any of the potentially important things that are presently taking place around me. I may miss information, that later may be essential to my survival. It is like putting a piece of chewing gum in the hole of a racing tire before you head out to the track.

cognitive maze

if i'm not really
worried about this
then why
do i keep
thinking
about it?

i split
the present tense
replay
the events
a quick anxiety fix
the perfect
defense

paradox of certainty
cognitivc maze
whatever it takes
to reclaim
my piece of mind

i won't let the past
repeat itself this time

Review

-the map is not the territory- Simply feeling the need to worry does not mean there is something to worry about. Just because people say they are going to do something, it doesn't mean they will.

-practicing imperfection- We are all imperfect and always will be. After all, life is presence in the expanding meaning. All we can do is use the most accurate map we have at any given time. Behaviors which have worked for us in the past may no longer be appropriate in the present. Conversely, behaviors may now find expression, which were at one time not well-received.

-depersonalizaton- Living through the eyes of my critics or admirers. Instead of relying on my own ability to take in and process the world, I choose to live up or down to the expectations of others.

-depression- When something must be given up in order to make room for something new. Depression is a natural reaction to having to give up a familiar part of myself.

time
frames

A "time frame" is a common example of framing. Setting a time frame of ten minutes for a meeting or exercise, for example, greatly influences what can be accomplished in that meeting. It determines where people will focus their attention, what topics and issues are appropriate for them to include in the interaction, and the type and degree of effort they will exert. A time frame of one hour or three hours for the same meeting or exercise would create quite different dynamics. Shorter time frames tend to focus people on tasks while longer time frames open up the possibility for people to also focus on developing relationships. If a time limit of 15 minutes has been set for a meeting, it is more likely that the meeting will be interpreted as being task-oriented rather than as an open-ended, exploratory brainstorming session.
-Robert B. Dilts

Time Frames

Time does not wait. Life is a series of adjusting to the times frames we are alloted at any given moment. The more time we have to reflect on our incoming perceptions the more closely in touch we become with the beliefs we attach to them. Think of a time frame as a box on a conveyer belt. Once a box is put on a conveyer belt there is a certain amount of time before another is put in front of that box, etc. Conversely, a box falls off the other end of the conveyer belt (thoughts becomes unconscious).

Understanding primary consciousness

My primary consciousness is the "I" or "Me" of my thoughts. Also, it is the amount of things I can keep within my immediate attention span at any one time. There are only so many things I can devote my attention to before I must make room for additional information.

Once upon a time a psychologist named George A. Miller attempted to measure the average working memory (capacity of our immediate attention span) by testing to see how many numbers a person can remember/retain in their focus at one time. Subjects were asked to look at a series of numbers and then told to recite how many they remembered. The average person was able to recall 7 numbers; this became known as the magical number seven of information processing.

The brain has a natural filtering mechanism. When it's operating properly new information flows in while simultaneously pushing out old information. It helped me a great deal to see the flow of my thinking in this way. The following model of consciousness helped me put it in perspective. Pay particular attention to the meaning of primary consciousness.

Conveyer Belt

Think of your Primary consciousness/immediate awareness as a series of boxes on a conveyer belt; that number of boxes may differ depending on how much incoming sensory information you must process. You can only hold so many things in your immediate awareness at one time. Once a new box is added to the conveyer belt, an old one falls off the end (into a level of unconsciousness/or can be recalled during reflective consciousness). There are several layers of consciousness.

Each new thought becomes the first or newest box on the conveyer belt. How long it stays on the conveyer belt is determined by how much time you are alloted to process it. In other words, each box is/has it's own time frame.

This was huge in helping me restore the balance to my thinking that OCD had so horribly confused. Understanding this helped me to resist to urge to be obsessive-compulsive. Simply by focusing on the new incoming box of information (living in the now/present moment) I was able to allow those obsessive-compulsive thoughts continue along the conveyer and fall into unconsciousness where they no longer had power over me. This, is THE HOW explanation to the JUST STOP suggestion, right here.

This book is nothing but a way to get you to expand your mind/thinking. The examples/poems/anecdotes I provide in the book are simply ways to get you to expand your ideas of what is possible within the realm of consciousness.

Here I provide a model of how to picture the conveyer belt process. Imagine the thoughts of an incoming box becoming replaced and falling off the end of the conveyer belt. Primary consciousness is where the box enters. Moreover, boxes may also enter from the side of the conveyer belt (periphery awareness). Also, they can be recalled back to the conveyer belt (reflective awareness).

G. William Farthing's Levels of consciousness model:

Primary Consciousness (What is happening in real time):

-Inner speech
-Mental images
-Feelings
-Attended sensory percepts
-Is the direct experience of percepts and feelings, and thoughts and memories arising in direct response to them. It is all includes spontaneously arising memories, thoughts, and images, including dreams and daydreams.

Reflective Consciousness:

-Self-awareness
-Introspection
-Consists of thoughts about one's own conscious experiences per se. In primary consciousness you are the subject who does the thinking, feeling, and acting in regard, mainly, to external objects and events. But in reflective consciousness your own conscious experiences - percepts, thoughts, feelings, and actions - are the objects of your thoughts.

Peripheral Awareness

-Stimuli vaguely aware
-info. in short-term memory
-Includes mental contents that are on the fringe of focal awareness. They can be brought into focal awareness almost instantaneously through either voluntary or involuntary (automatic) attention-switching processes. Peripheral awareness is at the border between conscious and nonconscious mind.

Levels of nonconscious mind
-High
-Medium
-Low
-None

Consider the following poem taking from the first book in my dark poetry series:

time frames

and so
life presses on
a series of
scattered conversations
lesser evils
and personal
invitations

small talk
politeness
life goes on
despite this
slightly witty
parade of
tainted sarcasm

no time to discuss
this thing
too busy
working
conversational
turn taking

if we are lucky
in the midst
of this
ever changing now
a smile or laugh
finds a way out
somehow
but mostly
we use
windows
of opportunity
to discuss the weather
or whatever

if love is a
mind virus
poets are doomed
to success
that is unless
it is words that cannot be
counted on
perhaps love is where
we can be found
our presence
and nothing more

Review

Time Frames- A time frame is the period of time I have to devote my attention to something or someone; it is short or long depending on the nature of the task at hand.

Primary Consciousness- My primary consciousness is the "I" or "Me" of my thoughts. Also, it is the amount of things I can keep within my immediate attention span. There are only so many things I can devote my attention to at one time.

Conveyer Belt- New boxes enter onto the conveyer belt at all times. Only so many boxes will fit on this conveyer belt until some must fall off the end in storage (unconsciousness).

the now

Trust that your memory works

Time really is everything and sometimes we have little or no control over how much reaction time we can give to a matter before it gets filed away into our memory. Often something will cue itself back from memory into our immediate awareness. It may even be a train of thought previously unfinished that we can now continue to focus on. The key to overcoming Anxiety and OCD lies within this very concept. You literally must TRUST that your memory functions properly enough for the process to occur. Our memory tends to work better when we trust in it. It's almost as if we have received an order for merchandise we have stored away in a warehouse. That cue or invoice reminds us of a previously unfinished thought. Our brains automatically take that invoice number into the wharehouse and find whatever is on the shelf next to that number. That literally is what memory is.

It's okay to reset our focus

We have to trust that every time we reset our focus we can always recall whatever it is we may have been thinking about during/after the reset/re-focus process. We, as OCD sufferers attempt to keep a great deal of things in our immediate consciousness at one time. The reason we do this is because we blame our supposedly poor memory for doing something wrong.

The now

The now is the present moment. It is everything you are experiencing at this instance in time. Right now that moment is being replaced with a new one and so forth. This process never stops. Part of understanding the conveyer belt phenomenon means understanding both the pro's and the con's of this very simple fact.

You can only keep so many things in your immediate awareness at one time. Let us look at an obsessive compulsive situation and how it relates to things that are happening in the now.

consistency

We are always attending to either external events or to daydreams, and short-term memory bridges the gaps between them. On rare occasions we may be shocked by what appreas to be a break in the continuity of consciousness. A typical case occurs in incidents of so-called "highway hypnosis." You may have had this experience while driving on a very familiar road or perhaps on a long straight highway, under easy driving conditions without much traffic, most likely at night. Suddenly you become aware that you have no recollection of having driven the last mile or so. You don't recall anything about the road or traffic or things along the way. What happened is that the simplicity of the driving task, at which you are highly practiced, enabled you to switch to 'autopilot," allowing automatic, nonconscious processes to do the driving. -William Farthing

Consciousness seeks an anchor

Our brains work like this naturally. This style of processing information makes us more efficient thinkers. Think of this process as having two conveyer belts at the same time.

Here, I have assigned a robot to the first conveyer belt (for a task that is mundane). This way I am able to attend myself to a second conveyer belt simultaneously (one which is also necessary or perhaps even more stimulating).

Hiring and firing autopilots

There are pros and cons to hiring an autopilot to any task. This is because the more in the moment I am when I initially experience something, the greater my capacity to recall it. Take the driving example given above. I will be able to recall little of the events which took place during the period I spent on auto-pilot.

The more in the moment I am when I initially experience something, the greater my ability will be to recall it. This concept is called **Anchoring**. Anchoring/choosing my auto-pilots well is essential for understanding how to beat OCD. I must be able to trust my memory; to trust myself. Memory distortion goes hand in hand with OCD (E.g. - Did I shut the oven off? Did I lock the front door before I went to bed?). Get in the habit of trusting your memory until trusting your memory in itself becomes automatic! Here is the consistency we need in our daily lives.

> Habits are functional because they simplify the movements required to achieve a result, increase the accuracy of behavior, reduce fatigue, and diminish the need to consciously attend to performed actions.

Anchoring

Anchoring is when a memory triggers a feeling that has repeatedly become associated with it. For example, the smell of spaghetti and meatballs brings you back to your childhood when your mother used to make them. There are constantly things that cue your memory and bring back feelings/sensations that were originally associated with them. Anchoring is the natural stamp made while establishing contact with the world. The power of contact always lies in the present. Contact is when we take the world in through our five senses and process that information through the filter of personal experience. This is where our habits begin!

Subconscious programming takes over the moment your conscious mind is not paying attention. The conscious mind can....think forward and backward in time, while the subconscious mind is always operating in the present moment....Nature did not intend the presence of the dual mind to be our Achilles heal. If our subconscious mind were programmed with....healthy behaviors, we could be totally successful in our lives without ever being conscious. -Bruce Lipton

Anchoring- Certain feelings/thoughts become associated with events as I experience them; these feelings and thoughts once experienced again, will cue the event back into awareness. The more I consciously devote my attention to something as I experience it, the better my chances will be to recall it back from memory.

Autopilot- When I decide to automatically do something without thinking about it so that I may consciously devote myself to something else at the same time.

Memory- If I am consciously present (and not on auto-pilot) while I experience an event, I will have a better chance of remembering it. When presented later with certain cues (feelings or thoughts that resulted from the event) I will be able to recall the event.

Habits- Things that I have perceived through anchoring and therefore, recalled accurately from memory. The prcoessing of this particular style of event has occured so many times, it has become unconscious.

landmarks for the cognitive map

The Law of Requisite Variety

> In plain terms this means that if you have more variety in your behavior than another person, then you can control your interactions with that person. For example, if your client George has five ways of resisting your good idea and you have enough variety in your behavior to deal effectively with each resistant move he makes, you should be able to control the outcome of your interactions with George. In other words, if you can make one more move than George can, you have requisite varity with respect to George. - Jerry Richardson

Basically, I have used the idea of the cognitive map to suggest that when certain experiences make an impression on us they become monumental. Whenever the feelings and memories associated with an event stand out, they serve as markers. A marker is an object used to indicate a position, place, or route. Why not collect as many useful markers as we can?

The first step in traveling anywhere involves knowing how to get there. If for instance, I want to vacation in Mexico, I must first decide where in Mexico I want to visit. Then, I must choose a mode of transportation. Furthermore, I can always consult a travel agent should I feel my options are limited. The point here is that it not does not hurt to be aware of other viewpoints.

The mean between two extremes

As a rule, the more variety I have in my behavior, the greater my opportunity to make contact with the people, places, and things in my world. This approach to understanding my interactions is not at all superficial or controlling. Quite the contrary, it helps me to keep myself in check.

The law of requisite variety suggests the importance of thinking outside the box. Indeed, just about any point of view has an opposite point of view. Not embracing one extreme does not mean I must embrace the other. Obviously, the more choices I have at my disposal, the less restricted I will be. My goal is to escape the prison of the black-or-white/all-or-nothing thinking that I have restricted myself to.

What makes the concept of 'The Highest Good' such a worthwhile one is that it contains within itself a blueprint for **how to JUST STOP** thinking a certain way. It not only says that I have an ultimate goal, it suggests how to re-position myself in respect to where I am, in order to achieve that goal.

I mentioned the concept of virtues before and how they are the mean between two extremes or opposites. It stands to reason I have many either-or patterns of thought I have restricted myself to.

I will use some conventional virtues as an example. Afterward, I will brainstorm and share some of my personal examples. At that point it will be up to you to identify and categorize your own. Earlier I mentioned Aristotle's concept of 'The Highest Good." As a rule, virtues are the balance between two opposing extremes. We will discover these virtues with our moral compass through the legitimate suffering of trial and error. And if our highest good is a worthy one it will require the discovery and mastery of many of these virtues along the way in order to achieve it.

I will list again the examples of virtues given by Aristotle, and also introduce a list of virtues provided by Erik Erikson.

Aristotle

Courage - (Cowardice/Rashness)
Temperance - (Insensibility/Intemperance)
Modesty - (Shamelessness/Bashfulness)
Right Ambition - (Want of Ambition/Over-ambition)
Wittiness - (Boorishness/Buffonery)
Sincerity - (Ironical Depreciation/Boastfulness)

Eric Erickson

Trust vs. Mistrust - Virtue: Hope
(Who is trustworthy and who isn't?)

Autonomy vs. Shame & Doubt - Virtue: Will
(Do my interests lead to self-sufficiency?)

Initiative vs. Guilt - Virtue: Purpose
(Am I good or bad?)

Industry vs. Inferiority - Virtue: Skill
(Does commitment to a goal pay off?)

Identity vs. Role Confusion - Virtue: Fidelity
(Who am I and where am I going?)

Intimacy vs. Isolation - Virtue: Love
(Am I loved for my ideas of right and wrong?)

Generativity vs. Stagnation - Virtue: Care
(Will I leave behind something of real value to the world?)

So what we have here so far is a basic template for a highest good. We'll call this template our cognitive map.

Highest Good

Mean
(Virtue)

Extreme		Extreme
Generativity	**Care**	Stagnation
Intimacy	**Love**	Isolation
Identity	**Fidelity**	Role Confusion
Industry	**Skill**	Inferiority
Initiative	**Purpose**	Guilt
Autonomy	**Will**	Shame & Doubt
Trust	**Hope**	Mistrust
Cowardice	**Courage**	Rashness
Insensibility	**Temperance**	Intemperance
Shamelessness	**Modesty**	Bashfulness
(Want of Ambition)	**Right Ambition**	Over-ambition
Boorishness	**Wittiness**	Buffonery
(Ironical Depreciation)	**Sincerity**	Boastfulness

(Starting point)

Can we construct our own virtues?

George Kelly took both the ideas of Aristotle and Erickson to a whole new level when he suggested (however unwittingly) that we also create our own virtues. He believed we all construct our own cognitions in the ways that we familiarize and contrast ourselves with the world (our own poles of opposite extremes for which we must find a balance).

We can be more flexible in our understanding of cognitions once we realize what these generalizations are. There is an entire constructivist psychology stemming from his work including 'The Journal of Constructivist Psychology,' which is specifically devoted to the theory. However, we need only look at his interpretation of anxiety and briefly relate it to his notion of constructs.

Whereas Freud considered wishes to be elements of the mind, Kelly proposed the idea of constructs. Constructs are a more specific way of categorizing the opposing extremes behind of our judgments and motivations. A construct is a way of distinguishing the difference between people and other people or an object and another object. A construct begins with at least two extreme positions (or poles) on either end of an issue. In addition, there can be three-pole constructs as. Together, all of these constructs represent a construction system.

The stand-up comedy of George Carlin can provide us with an amusing way of understanding and remembering this concept of a construct. Carlin once commented that he tends to categorize drivers in either of two categories: "Anyone driving slower than me is an idiot, and anyone driving faster than me is a maniac," he said.

I think my dad has personally adopted this construct because even twenty years after we first heard this together he still alludes to the comment, and often confesses that he feels the same way. The point is that he has a tendency to construct driving behavior within two opposing extremes, or categories. And if a person is not one, they are the other: idiot - maniac.

We construct these two-pole extremes all the time in daily life yet we rarely notice it. In fact, if we meet a person that seems to embody both sides of the poles of one of our constructs we may accuse them of being a hypocrite, when in reality it may be only our subjective judgment that is skewed. I have noticed a stunning example of this in one of my own constructs about driving.

Once when I was eighteen I was pulled over on the Atlantic City expressway for driving in the passing lane while there were no cars on the road. Baffled, I listened to the officer as she reminded me that in the driver's manual the DMV specifically instructs us to use the passing lane for passing and the cruising lane for cruising. "If there is no one on the road" she said, "you don't need to be in the passing lane do you?"

Well, sometimes I wish this had never happened to me because I basically agreed with the officer, and for a long time afterwards I harbored a strong dislike for anyone that I felt was "cruising" in the passing lane. I would get especially angry at those people who I felt who were impeding the flow of traffic by not letting those of us pass who wanted to. My driving construct for many years was passing vs. not passing. And my behavior was congruent with this belief. I always made sure to move out of the way of other drivers who had a greater sense of urgency than me; because this was the way I had constructed reality. Moreover, I felt this constructed reality had been validated and so it remained unchallenged, for a long time. After all, I got it straight from a police officer!

Interestingly, my stepfather has a driving construct that is quite different from mine. He points out that the driving manual states that there is to be no passing on right, regardless as to whether he is passing someone in the passing lane or not. He has developed a construct that is congruent with this belief; and he respects the rights of others in the same regard. He will not pass people on the right, etc.

After thinking about this and remembering certain conversations that I've had with people throughout the years, I began to realize that my stepfather had an interesting point; and it seemed to explain the gap in my understanding as to why some people clog up the passing lane. In fact, I realized that most likely our opposing arguments were representative of two of the major arguments that people have about driving! Of course, some people just don't care either way, and perhaps they don't pay attention whatsoever.

Hence, I now have a new, modified (three-pole) construct: **There are some people who believe the passing lane is only for passing - there are those who believe you should not pass on the right even if you aren't passing - and those who really don't care or pay attention to either of these things.**

The funny thing is that I get less angry on the road now. I have more respect for other drivers. I am less willing to risk an accident in order to teach someone a tail-gating lesson about the passing lane! And I am less likely to race by somebody on the right in order to get in front of them. Of course, this whole matter may just be an indication that there is a flaw in the driver's manual. Or more importantly, it could be an indication that my construction system was not working for me. The point is: this new construct works, at least for now. It has helped me to have more of an open mind as to the motivations of others - and even more importantly - it keeps me out of trouble.

This kind of neatly sums up not only Kelly's idea of the poles of constructs, but also his definition of anxiety as well. For Kelly, anxiety is created when your construction system does not adequately depict reality for you, and as a result you don't respond well to it. Suddenly, you may find yourself in a situation where your construction system does not provide an appropriate course of action for you. As a result, your anxiety flares up and you may turn inwards by withdrawing into a more stereotyped, constricted type-of-compliance.

The following are some other examples and the opposite extremes that underlie them. I drew these up as further examples. Again, any and all scaffolds (concepts borrowed) must be processed through personal experience.

Neurotics vs. Character Disorder

> Most people who come to see a psychiatrist are suffering from what is called either a neurosis or a character disorder. Put most simply, these two conditions are disorders of responsibility, and as such they are opposite styles of relating to the world and its problems. The neurotic assumes too much responsibility; the person with a character disorder not enough. When neurotics are in conflict with the world they automatically assume that they are at fault. When those with character disorder are in conflict with the world they automatically assume that the world is at fault. -Scott Peck

Finding that balance

Those who are neurotic tend to blame themselves for everything. Those who are psychotic tend to blame everyone else. Clearly there are some of us who fall on one end of either extreme. Most of us, however, fall somewhere else along this continuum. The point is that some things in life are our responsibility and some things simply are not. Moreover, what we feel is and is not our responsibility may at times conflict with what another person feels is or is not our responsibility. This, like everything else in life is a balance which must be explored first-hand and mastered if we are to successfully navigate ourselves into a healthier state of being.

> Most examples of compulsive checking are attempts to prevent a misfortune, however obscure. The person strives for certainty that no harm will occur to others because of his negligence or supposedly poor memory. "I must check at least ten times to be absolutely sure that the stove is off and will not cause a deadly fire." The drive to check repeatedly is intended if and when the person feels solely or largely responsible for safety, for example if he is the last peron to leave the house or office. -De Sliva and Rachman

Inflated sense of responsibility

OCD is considered to be a neurosis. Many of us who suffer through anxiety attempt to carry the weight of the world on our shoulders. We take on responsibility for things which we have little or no control over. A great deal of ritualistic behavior is spent on trying to prevent some kind of misfortune to ourselves or others.

The above example suggests an all-or-nothing style of thinking (check the stove ten times or there may be a fire). OCD is an amazing collection of such irrational connections of cause and effect. Again, there is almost always more than two-opposing extremes to consider. The following is a poem which I use as anecdote for explaining the importance of finding the various angles behind something and breaking free of the all-or-thing chains of thinking which bind us.

angles

no one
is against you
they call it psychosis
this isn't about
you
either
so just take
a breather

just because you
disagree it
doesn't
make you wrong
not loving your
weakness
doesn't make you strong

if having the widest
range of
responses
is part of the plan
collect as
many viewpoints
as you can
everyone
is a little mean
it shows character

IQ vs. Emotional Intelligence

> Academic intelligence offers virtually no preparation for the turmoil - or opportunity life's vicissitudes bring. Yet even though a high IQ is no guarantee of prosperity, prestige, or happiness in life, our schools and our culture fixate on academic abilities, ignoring emotional intelligence, a set of traits - some might call it character - that also matters immensely for our personal destiny. Emotional life is a domain that, as surely as math or reading, can be handled with greater or lesser skill, and requires its unique set of competencies.
> -Daniel Goldman

The emotionally intelligent are capable of feeling what others are feeling. They are empathetic in every sense of the word and excel in the art of relationships. Whether they are organizing groups, negotiating solutions, or preventing personal conflicts these people are natural leaders.

The ability to detect the motivations of others will strongly determine the success rate of almost any career path. After all, you can have a high IQ and still be an axe-murderer. Death row is full of anti-social prodigies. Even though you got that high-paying job that all your perfect grades won you, can you excel at it within the organizational structure? Do you have the social/emotionally intelligent skills necessary to lead and work your way up the ranks?

logic is the enemy

not important
we understand
what comes
from our heads
we teach to the test
no arrested
development
or emotional
intelligence

not important
to know
we sub-communicate
nor is recess
important anyway

if it's valid then say it
if direct enough
convey it
conclusions built
on premises
portray it

somewhere today
is a genius
on death row

Contact vs. Confluence

> The opposite of contact is "confluence," acting out of what you have been taught to do, out of habit, or seeing things as you "should" be seeing a work of modern art. He feels he is directly perceiving the work, when in fact "he is actually in contact with the art critic of his favorite journal."
> -(Miriam and Erving Polster)

Confluence can be seen in relationships where a couple looks to avoid argument or confrontation. Likewise, there tends to be a tacit agreement between both partners not to rock the boat (or address certain issues). After a failed marriage both parties may express a general lack of acknowledgement that there were any problems at all. "We almost never argued, in the entire time we knew each other," they may exclaim. In some cases a need to not be lonely may overwhelm the need for compatibility in which case they develop more of a superficial or co-dependent relationship.

the defense mechanism of confluence

agreed to disagree
the contract
has been signed
the me
i won't resign
has not yet
given up
it's simply
lost within us

at some point
halves
become a whole
i love you
like confluence
the lack
of discord
we influence

Moving beyond the provided examples

I have provided many examples of opposite extremes. All of these concepts may serve as a scaffold for you until you develop your own. Again, what you discover through the eyes of the critic are at the end of the day, derived from someone else's impressions and ideas. Ultimately, you must take them in through the first person and process them through your filter of individuality. See what kind of cognitive map you can briefly sketch of your own.

Highest Good

Mean
(Virtue)

Extreme   **Extreme**

Starting Point

Crystallized Intelligence

The concept of Crystallized Intelligence was introduced by psychologist Raymond Cattell. Crystallized intelligence is how we describe a set of skills which are a direct result of practice and experience. For example, I studied psychology for several years in college. Even though I was given several lectures and taught several fascinating things from reading books and doing homework assignments, the real learning took place through actual pattern recognition and first-hand experiences with the concepts.

Indeed, you are being introduced to a number of concepts which may be new to you. As a result it may take time to breathe these ideas in and filter them through your own personal experience. Then and only then will this information have crystallized.

Review

The law of requisite variety- the ability to consider more than one angle to a matter.

IQ vs. Emotional Intelligence- IQ is a way of measuring academic achievement: verbal comprehension, perceptual speed, intellectual capacity, etc. Emotional Intelligence involves coping skills, leadership qualities, capacity for empathy, and other interpersonal skills.

Neurotics vs. Character Disorder- Neurotics/thos with anxiety blame themselves for everything. Those with character disorders/psychotics blame the world.

Inflated Sense of Responsibility- the tendency of those with OCD to carry the weight of the world on their shoulders and think they can prevent harm to others by carrying out obsessive-compulsive rituals.

Contact vs. Confluence- The mean between living in the now and taking in the world through my five senses and basing who I am by what my critics say about me.

Crystallized Intelligence- The information you have taken in first through pattern recognition must be filtered through personal experience for it to have real meaning in your life: Practice makes perfect. It is your own brand of the concepts lent to you from the world (tried and true).

notes

works cited

David Lester, Theories Of Personality: A System's Approach (Bristol, Pennsylvania: Taylor & Francis, 1995).

Alfred Korzybski, Science and Sanity fifth edition (Englewood, New Jersey, USA: Insititute Of General Semantics, 1994).

L. Nathan Oaklander, Existentialist Philosophy An Introduction (Englewood Cliffs, New Jersey: Prentice-Hall, Inc., 1992).

Richard Brodie, Virus of the mind the new science of the meme (Seattle: Integral Press, 1996).

Jerry Richardson, The Magic Of Rapport (Capitola, CA: Meta Publications, 2000).

Daniel Goleman, Emotional Intelligence (Broadway, New York, New York: Bantam Books, 1995).

Padmal De Silva, Stanley Rachman Obsessive-Compulsive Disorder The Facts Third Edition (New York: Oxford University Press, 2004).

M. Scott Peck, M.D., The Road Less Traveled (New York, NY: Touchstone, 2003).

Jose A. Yaryura-Tobias, M.D., F.A.C.P.M., Fugen A. Neziroglu, PH.D, A.B.B.P., A.B.P.P. Obsessive-Compulsive Disorder Spectrum Pathogenesis, Diagnosis, and Treatment (Washington, DC: American Psychiatric Press, Inc., 1997).

Robert D. Enright, Phd, Forgiveness is a choice (Washington, DC: APA Life Tolls American Psychological Association, 2001).

Diane E. Papalia, Sally Wendkos Olds, Ruth Duskin Feldman, A child's world Infancy Through Adolescence Tenth Edition (New York, NY: McGraw-Hill, 2006).

Jeffrey M. Schwartz, MD with Beverly Beyette, Brain Lock (New York, NY: Harper Collinsbooks, 1996).

Gerald Nierenberg and Henry H. Calero How to read a person like a book (New York, NY: Pocket Books, a division of Simon & Schuster, Inc., 1971).

Erving Polster, Ph.D. and Miriam Polster, Ph.D. Gestalt Therapy Integrated (New York: Vintage Books edition, 1974).

Dr. Nicky Hayes, Teach Yourself: Psychology (Chicago, IL: Contemporary Books, a Division of the McGraw Hill companies, 2003).

Gail Steketee, Ph.D., Teresa Pigott, M.D. Obsessive Compulsive Disorder The latest assessment and treatment strategies (Kansas City, MO: Compact Clinicals, 2006).

David Silverman, Harvey Sacks Social Science & Conversation Analysis (Cambridge CB2 1 UR, UK: Polity Press, Oxford OX 41JF: Blackwell Publishers Ltd, 1998).

Bruce H. Lipton, PH.D., The Biology Of Belief (New York, NY: Mountain of Love Productions, 2008).

Steven J. Luck, An Introduction To The Event-Related Potential Technique (Cambridge, Massachusetts Institute of technology, 2005).

B.R. Hergenhahn, An Introduction to the History of Psychology fifth edition (Toronto, Ontario: Wadsworth, a division of Thomson Learning, 2005).

Gregory Bateson, Steps to an Ecology of Mind (Chicago, IL: The University Of Chicago Press, 1972).

G. William Farthing, The Psychology of Consciousness (Upper Saddle River, NJ: Prentice Hall, 1992).

Judith Rapoport, M.D., The Boy Who Couldn't Stop Washing (New York, NY: Plume, 1990).

William James, The Principles of Psychology (New York, NY: Dover Publications, Inc., 1918).

Ian Jakes, Theoretical Approaches to Obsessive Compulsive Disorder (New York, NY: Cambridge University Press, 1996). Robert B. Dilts, Sleight of Mouth (Capitola, California: Meta Publications, 1999).

Rick Warren, The Purpose Driven Life (Grand Rapids, Michigan: Zondervan, 2002).

David DeAngelo's Sexual Communication and Power Sexuality were referenced in this book. I highly recommend both of these publications, as well as interviews with dating gurus, where David D talks directly with Tyler Durden.

Victor Frankl, Man's Search For Meaning (New York, NY: Touchstone: A trademark of Simon & Schuster, Inc., 1984).

Victor Frankl, The Will To Meaning (New York, NY: Meridian- Penguin Books, 1988).

Robert B. Dilts, Sleight Of Mouth (Capitola, California 95010: Meta Publications, 1999).

Frank def productions

other
books
by
Frank
DeF

the dark poetry series

available on amazon.com www.createspace.com and www.frankdefproductions.com

The first book in the series:

Vol 1- Here We Reach The Beginning

The subgenre known as Dark Poetry: Finding inspiration from tragedy & darkness. Often it is when things do not go our way and life is difficult that we become motivated to achieve more than ever. Sometimes spiritual growth requires us to embrace our dark side in order to make sense of our suffering. This book is about that journey within, into the darkness, and our very return

Vol 2 - Death is in my coffee

     Those dark, hidden aspects of our being that tend to control our motivations if we remain unaware of their existence. The premise behind "Death is in my Coffee" and the entire Dark Poetry series is based upon the idea of the 'the shadow' as proposed by Carl Jung. The idea is that if we embrace our dark side (bring the hidden aspects of ourselves into awareness) we are in a better position to notice and improve those unwanted or harmful aspects of our personality that pull our strings, unconsciously.

Vol 3 - Deeper Now

     Takes a greater plunge into dark erotica while also exploring dark lore and myth. The idea behind the book is similar to the first two: finding inspiration from tragedy.. and embracing the previously hidden aspects of ourselves.. The writing provides a 'reflective interpretation.' In other words, you will perceive the message of the poems as being positive or negative depending on what is going on inside you.

Currently, my books are being circulated through detention centers, shelters, and hospitals. I also donate to veterans and troops abroad.

I am always interested in donating books to a worthy cause.

for more information
email me
at

speedingcamaro@gmail.com

Stop by and see me on my website:

www.frankdefproductions.com

Made in the USA
Columbia, SC
13 August 2023

21545398R00065